Trigger Warning

This book explores content based on mental health, sexual abuse, addiction, trauma, recovery, and more. It is not written in attempts to romanticize these topics, whatsoever. This is purely based on my own story and experience.

With love and intentions of healing,

  Charlie Iris

A Letter to My Lover

Charlie Iris

Dive into the wounds of a poet who fell in love with a Leo. Follow the one year journey of battling traumatic flashbacks, psych ward admissions, and becoming a fur mum, all while loving someone fighting an internal war, too. This is a modern day love story that looks an awful lot like a slightly twisted fairytale. 'A Letter to My Lover' is written as a love letter, with each poem placed in chronological order, that turns out to be a final good-bye. Brace yourself, sit back, and enjoy.

A Letter to My Lover

contents

7	To The Love Of My Life
8	Learning To Eat Again
10	Searching for You, Lover
11	The Night I Met the Love of My Life
13	Icarus On Your Arm
14	Today's the Day for Bettering You
16	Soul Mates
17	Out Loud
19	All Of The Ways I Know I Love You
21	Meet Me Halfway
24	For the Very First Time
25	Bungalow
28	Moving Day
29	Just A Little Bit of Hope
30	Silence In A Kiss
32	Dizzy Thoughts
34	Shapeshifting

By Charlie Iris

A Letter to My Lover

contents

37	Rational Breathing
39	My Point Always Gets Lost
43	To Be His Lioness
45	The Attic
47	Tuesdays at 5
50	Cat Mum
52	Sweet 16
55	Duck Tube Socks
57	To the Boy Who Can't Even Butter His Own Toast
59	The R Word
61	Silence is Wishful Thinking
62	Metal Spoons
63	Let's Talk About the Psych Ward
66	Regret
67	Nightmares From Another Realm
68	Engagement Nails
69	Failing Mindfulness

By Charlie Iris

A Letter to My Lover

contents

70	All of These Are Written In Marker
71	Patience
72	A Wishful Goodnight
73	Recreate
74	Home At Last
75	Rose Bush
76	Karma's A Bitch, & So Are You
77	Seamless
79	Counting Sheep
81	Growing Into Myself
84	Dear Mother, I'm Sorry
86	Survivor
89	Discrete
90	Realization
92	A Million Times
94	Perceptive Wisdom
95	Depression Snack

By Charlie Iris

A Letter to My Lover

contents

98 Skint

99 I Do

103 Sticky Notes: The Continuum

105 Naming The Dead

106 When Nobody Answers

107 Warning Label

109 One Week Later

110 Even If You Walk Away

112 Let Me Read You

113 Always Wait It Out

By Charlie Iris

To The Love Of My Life

I cut my hair,
I know you'd like it.
I paint my nails,
I know you wouldn't mind it.
I sing the same song over and over,
And you'll sing along in defeat.

I don't know you yet,
But I love you.
I love you so much already, that
I'm not lonely because I'm not with you;
I'm complete because I know you're
Out there on your way to me.

I'll love the way "I love you,"
Rolls off your tongue and onto mine.
I'll love the way our babies have
Your eyes.
I'll love the way you say my name,
And for it to link with your last.

I love nothing more
Than the love you have yet to offer me.

Learning To Eat Again

I have starved myself for love,
Yet I learned how to feast on the feeling.
I have cut lines in my arms and legs
For a story I never wanted to write,
But I learned how to heal the wounds
By my own care.
I have walked through forests
And swam through oceans, just
To learn how to find myself.

All of this learning and I'm not even a student,
But the lessons follow me wherever I go.
There are days when the only thing
Keeping me alive is the fear that
I wouldn't do it right: end it.

But then I think of my children, the ones
I have yet to bear, and how their
Starving eyes will gaze back at mine
And how precious that moment will be.
I daydream over how their laughs
Will sound, and how mine will harmonize
With their innocents.

Recently, I haven't thought too much
About ending it. I haven't written more
Lines either in three months.
So maybe things are picking up-
Maybe the sunrise is an image
I'm more willing to look at.
Maybe the sky is more blue
Because I painted it that way.
Maybe fruit tastes more sweet
Because I planted their seeds.
Whatever the reason,
I'm willing to eat more.
No longer will I starve myself for love.

Searching For You, Lover

(October 15th, 2020)

I'm tired of wondering where you are.
Wondering if you're with her instead of
Me. Wondering if you're telling her
You love her instead of me.
Wondering what's taking you so damn
Long to catch up to me.
You see, I've ran away for so many years,
That I need to slow down in order for you
To reach me.
I love you.
Can't you understand?
I'm waiting for you.
I'm begging for you.
I'm praying for you.
Every night when I see the first star

Come out in the sky,
I wish for you.
My heart aches because you're not with me.
You don't even know me.
I don't even know you.
But for so many reasons and more,
I love you.

The Night I Met the Love of My Life

(October 22, 2020)

Sticking to the car's seat
In sweat from nerves I've never felt before,
Which says something coming from
A lass with an anxiety disorder.
I collect myself with one deep breath
And exit the car into the brisk autumn
Air. My wobbly knees make their way
To the bar. The door opens and
A girl greets me with a smile.
Suddenly, I'm struck with awe
As I hear your hands strumming
Your guitar and your voice booming
Through the building.
I turn to you, we smile, my heart does
A little jig, and I think I feel yours dancing
With mine too. I take a seat, and
Embarrassingly never take my eyes off you
Until yours are glued on me.
I could write a whole book solely based on the
Night we first met,
But I'll keep this as short as I can.
We discuss your 10 month vacation,
Our tattoos,
Greek mythology, and everything in between
Here, the sky, and the ocean.
Your best friend carries the conversation
For the rest of the night; high as a kite
And spilling more than I'm sure he cares to
Admit. I tell him there has to be something
Wrong with you, because you're too

Good to be true. He doesn't even crack a
Smile. Instead, he agrees and tells me
That there's a lot more than what meets
The eye. It doesn't scare me. I have demons
Too. As disturbed as it may sound,
I can't wait for you to introduce me to
Those demons of yours.
By the end of the night, I decide
I'm not here just to meet you.
I'm here to know you.
So if that means 40 minute drives
With my skin sticking to
My leather seats with nervous sweats,
Then so be it.

Icarus On Your Arm

I should've turned my car around.
I should've called you from the bottom of
your stairs
And waited for you to come down to them.
And then, I should've kissed you-
For many reasons.

1: I wanted to thank you.

2: I wanted to take any pain away that you might have.

3: I wanted to show you that I see you, I hear you, I'm not going anywhere.

It doesn't
Scare me, and by "it," I mean your past.
I don't know the shadows that lurk
In your corner.
I don't know them by their names,
Their faces, or their actions.
But I see them. I feel them.

I want you to know that
You don't have to hide it;
For our shadows can dance together.
I want to fly in between the sun, and
In between the ocean.
May our wings never melt or
Deteriorate.

Today's the Day for Bettering You

You're the one
I've been dreaming of.
You're the one I have been
Wishing all of my lucky stars on.
You're the one that makes all
Of the love songs mean something.
You're the one that makes life
Mean something again.
It pains me to know you're in pain,
But don't take that the wrong way.
Understand that I am honoured to
Be able to be so vulnerable with you
About our demons and
All of the terrors we faced.
Today, and every day, my love,
I will thank God for you.
I have fallen in love with you so fast
And smoothly that I thought I was
Slipping on a banana peel.
Your goal every day is to make me
Laugh or at least smile twice a day,
But hunny, you exceed every time, no
Matter the mood.
Making love with you is so passionate.
I swear, water from earth's finest
Glaciers are envious of our purity.
Love with you is love in its simplest form.
It is there, just like those shadows that
Follow you everywhere.
You're so brave, my love.
You're so honest and brutal, at that-
I wouldn't have you any other way.

Today is the start of our journey to
Bettering your mental health.
So take my hand,
Let me guide you into this hospital,
Let them ask you a million questions
And answer with your raw thoughts.
I cannot wait to hold you close and tell
You how proud I am of you.
My baby, how proud I am that no matter
The ugly that you face, you turn
Everything you touch into magnificent beauty.

Soul Mates

I wrote poems about you
Before even knowing of your
Existence.
I craved your kiss
Before even tasting your
Lips.
I missed your heartbeat
Before even knowing its
Rhythm.

You are everything I've ever dreamed of.
All of the good, the bad, the sweet and sour.
You are the one I've been searching
Night and day for; hiking trails beyond
Forests and mountains.
You are the answer to my prayers;
The luckiest of stars I ever wished upon.

Waking up used to
Be my least favourite part
Of the day.
The realization of existing
Another day would hit harder
Than a fourth shot of tequila.
But now that I wake up next to you,
It's my favourite part of every day.
I get to hear "good morning,
beautiful,"
I get to snuggle you, and I get to
Invision the next few decades
doing the
Exact same thing.
Waking up next to you is the best
Dream of all.

Out Loud

All of the ways I can say
"I love you," remain silent;
Trapped in my mouth like moths
Stuck on double sided tape.
I love how you hold me close.
It's as though you're trying to
Put back all of our broken pieces.
Our pieces fit perfectly together like
A puzzle that has been in the building
Process for 22 years.
I love that we have a future as one.
I love that our children will have our
Sparkling blue eyes, with your rosy cheeks
And maybe my dimples.
I love how your thoughts align with mine.
I love how your smile bursts from
Ear to ear and lights up the entire universe
With just one smirk.
I love that you impulsively bought a coffee
Maker at 5AM, so we can have a cuppa
That's not made in the microwave.
I love that you love that I started to
Feed the cats even though they're
Technically not mine.

I love that you kiss me when I'm asleep
And I somehow kiss you back even though
I'm out cold.
I love that you hate when I leave
My wet towel on the bed sheets, and
How you don't get mad that I've
Forgotten and done it
Again for the hundredth time.
My love, I'm sorry I'm unable to
Communicate so fluently the way you do.
My love language is foreign and
Nonsensical to anyone who dare listen-
But you, you listen even though it doesn't
Make sense. You help me learn my own
Words and rearrange them until they form
A proper sentence.
You never get frustrated with me.
You never judge me.
You never give up on me.
You are everything I have ever dreamed of,
And I mean that with my whole heart.
In due time, I will tell you these things
Out loud.

All of The Ways I Know I Love You

I've gotten used to sleeping in subzero
Temperatures, even though I hate it.
But now if the window is open in the midst
Of January, I don't immediately close it-
Instead, I leave it open. I let the downtown
Street lights engulf my senses; almost
Tasting their amber brightness.
I leave it open despite my chattering
Bones, because I know you overheat
At night and I want you to get a good rest.

Even though I
Have forgotten about my freshly used
Towel laying on the bed
Again, you still love me; which makes
Me love you more because I know it's
An annoying habit of mine, yet you accept
It anyway.

That's the thing about you: you accept me.
You get my quirks, laugh at my odd numbers
In even equations, and
Helped me become a better version
Of myself that just needed a little guidance
To shine through.

When you tell me you love me,
I say I love you back, but I say it as though
I'm almost boasting about it.
Like fuck yea, I love you! You and only
You. So why not be proud of that?

Waking up beside you is the best
Part of every day, and something I get
Butterflies from at night as I fall
Asleep.

Basically, every atom of mine loves every
Atom of yours.

Respectfully speaking, you are mine
And I am yours.

Meet Me Halfway

If someone would have told younger
Me about future you, us;
I would've laughed in their face and called
Them a liar.

You see, you are perfect for me.
If I were to play SIMS, I would
Build a character just like you.
Handsome, flirtatious, and talented.
What more could I ask for? Yet somehow,
There's more!

You are the most beautiful soul
I have ever come in contact with.
You're free-spirited, bold, courageous,
And everything I ever could've dreamed of,
Physically speaking.

Sometimes you don't see your own beauty
Or worth and I become upset with the
World again.
I just wish the demons in your head
Could find another place to torment.
I wish you health when the time is right,

And you pray for me nightly.
If only there was a way for me to
Take away your pains and sorrows,
To replace them with gains and better
Tomorrow's.

I'm of the jealous kind, and trembled
When the weed hit and the girl wouldn't
Stop rambling.
"I know his birthday," her snarky tone spat,
Interrupting my forgetfulness.
All I wanted to do in that moment was to
Stumble home with you.

Home to bed, the two cats, the dishes.
I wanted to go home to the loft
I've filled with plants.
But I was sat there like a boneless
Chicken: a little wobbly and without
A backbone to lean on. But instead, I
Listened to her rant, giggled when she
Wasn't looking at the eye rolls you'd make,
And I fell in love with your loyalty.
Your eyes were on me. Only. As my eyes
Were on you. Only.

You are the me I had lost some time ago.
You are the best thing to happen to me,
Since I was first deemed worthy enough
To not get picked on at school.
You are the protector I knew was looking
Out for me from afar.
You are the Prince Charming I would make
All of my Barbie's fall in love with as a kid.

If someone would've told younger me
That you were on your way to love me,
And be in love with me, then I probably
Would've laughed in their face

And politely ask them in which direction
You're headed from, so I could meet you
Halfway.

For The Very First Time

I believe I see a piece of
Heaven when I look
Into his eyes.
Whispering hues of blue, green and yellow-
Strike a familiar chord within me.
It's like these pods of an endless daydream,
Are simply my habitat called home.
I live in them.
My being is there within them,
As he looks at me.
I can see my own reflection among the
Vibrant colours of his iris':
My frail and gentle self is isolated against
The icy saturation.

Someday, our babies will have eyes like
That- bold enough to make a
Plan come to life, yet puppy enough
They can make big girls cry.
I'll find truth behind their innocents,
And joy beyond the sadness shown too.
They'll have bluebells for eyes, as their
Whole being is a wildflower field.
I cannot wait to find my reflection
In their eyes too.
For when I had seen it in yours,
It was like I saw myself
For the very first time.

Bungalow

Pulling out of the driveway
To the place I called home.
Mother waves bye-bye and
Father says hold on.
I cannot stay any longer,
I've overstayed my welcome.
You've done so much for me,
It's time I show you I can do it from here,
But please don't stop checking in.

The window to my old bedroom is blacked
Out by the lack of sun and life
Between its walls. Peace falls over me
As I think, "Maybe those memories were
Painted over and I'll never have to see them
Again."
Those memories are ones I fight hard
To keep underwraps. Maybe now
That I won't be sleeping in that room
Every night, they can willow away
Like I have in self-pity,
After realizing what he made of me.
The thing is, I have built myself
Back up from the crumbled ashes
You crisped me into. I am thriving,
I am whole. I am two halves of a broken
Soul that was mended by love.
I watered each chakra until I was
Aligned again.
I fed myself until I purged; repeated,
So I'd never feel empty.

It is so strange that somewhere with so many
Happy memories, has been tarnished
By an oil spill such as him.
Christmas morning surprises and cuddles
With my parents in bed,
Are far from the present.
Birthdays and laughter from friends that
Have come and gone,
Still echo under each rug in the house.
Footprints from visiting guests have
Since been swept up and replaced by
Others.
My mother is a deep cleaner, so I pray
That she scrubbed each inch clean from
His dirty embodiment.
If she hasn't, I promise, that I will
Remove it myself if I see one speck of
Him still there.

Bungalow,
Sweet and small.
I crave the sensation of
Letting him go, and falling into the abyss,
To which he'd never break free from.
Bungalow,
Sometimes I dream of you
Burning to the ground and the horrors
I faced inside, burned to the ground too.
But there is so much more
To that house than what I remember so
Vividly. There is so much more there than

Pain, questions with no answers, and
Heartache without the power to make them look twice.
Bruising from blows I've taken by the wind,
Beating me blue until I am sore.
Bubbles, puppies, and grief all in one picture,
Right outside that bungalow.

Dear bungalow, I hope we can make amends.
For you are not the one who has sinned.

Moving Day

I'll make these four walls a home;
That's my promise to you.
Sure, it's going to be tough for a while,
But nobody can say we aren't trying.
So let's pack all of our belongings,
Try our best to hold back from crying,
And carry on through the day.
This is a new, big, scary, exciting
Chapter and I'm so glad you're part of it.
I wouldn't want anyone else but you.
It may not be much,
But it's what we've got-
Remember that it isn't all we've got.
We may not have much, but at least it's
Ours.

Just a Little Bit of Hope

I am hopeful for the future.
For one day, tomorrow was the day I met you.
For when I thought I'd take my last breath,
I took another.
For when I got lost,
You found me and took me home.

Silence in A Kiss

Blood is dripping,
Circling the drain.
Hands shaking,
Heart pumping fast.
My hands shake,
My vision blurs.

You twist the doorknob
And let out a breath.
Your hands break the tension
Between my fingers and the razor.
You check my arms. Nothing.
No cuts, no blood; I imagined it all.
The sink is empty. The mirror is not,
As my trembling lip meets my eyes
In the reflection.
You pull me closer to the door. I step over
The picture you drew for me;
Roses below my feet. The petals are
Intact but I am not.
The blue ink fades from my mind as I take
My place against the bedroom wall.
You insist that I take a seat on the bed,
But my dear, I'm afraid that if I do, it
Will swallow me whole.
I take my chances anyway. Your arms wrap
Around me and you sob.
I'm so sorry for the fear I caused. The panic
Was unfair of me to load onto you.

My mind takes me back to the bathroom
Where the blood in my mind still sits
In the sink.
How do I put down the blade when it feels
Like I'm a magnet that has met its match?
My thoughts hollow my brain until
There is nothing left but mush.
I cannot process the words you are speaking
Right now.
These thoughts are so much
Louder than your voice.

Please don't hate me.
Please don't doubt me.
Please don't leave me.

Before I know it, I'm wrapped in your
Robe and placed on the bed.
My eyes shut.
You kiss my forehead, and
The world stops being loud for all the time
Your lips are pressed to my flesh.

Dizzy Thoughts

Cold season is constant
When working at a daycare.
My immune system has always been shit,
So I'm sick once again.

This time, things are different.
Things are more comfortable and
Loving.
Instead of being told that I'm gross
And not kissable,
You shower me in golden
Sweet *I love you*'s

I'm left wondering why
I had put up with so much.
Why being cut down like a tree
That was persistent to grow past its
Upturned roots, wasn't enough for me
To just replant myself somewhere else?

Why did I let my burning star burn out?
Why did she not fly past the others in the sky?
Why did she have to die?

Why did my brother and sister not
Blink an eye,
When I uncovered the truth
Behind their unaware minds?

My nose is dripping;
Making me feel more ill than a dog.
My skin sweats as I pant above the
Bedsheets in this February weather.

I see you at the end of the bed.
My missing puzzle piece in this jumbled
Box of life.
I want your arms near and tight.
But I fear I am too gross for you now,
So I stay away in slight fear.
Because I wasn't enough before,
So why wouldn't that mean I'm still
Not enough now?
Someone please give me a pain killer,
For being sick is far beyond just having a cold.

Shapeshifting

Reflections have always been funny
To me:
Time frozen still long enough that
I can stare a little before disappearing.

Not even a mirror finds worth in carrying
My reflection.
It distorts it, in hopes I never turn back
And look twice.

I wonder what they see in me, if anything
At all. Maybe that's why I vanish into
Thin air when I try to stand tall.

Why must I always disappear?

I'm just trying to find density
In all of this mass.
Trying to fit inside small spaces:
I fold myself up, hunch my back, suck
In my belly, to take
Up less room.

No wonder my stomach always aches.
Trying to form abs I haven't had
In years-
And daydreaming of checking
My reflection before exiting my bedroom,
To see if I was thin enough to go to the kitchen and eat.

High school is the best years of your life.
Granola bars on my desk
And tucked away in a binder.
Almost fainting every day and
Skipping class to find sharp objects to dwindle
Away at my own wrists.
How can someone be so cruel to
Themselves?

Peroxide and bandages used to be
My partner in crime.
I haven't done it in almost
A year, so maybe that's an improvement.
Or maybe I've just gotten tired of
Taking care of each cut until a new one appeared next to it.

There was a time when my wrists wrote more stories
Than my pencils ever did,
But I'm writing my own book, and
This chapter is on paper.
This chapter has kitten whiskers,
Ginger beards, and roses.
So do not fear for me, or fear of me.
Please know I am just getting all of my
Story out there.
Please know he is taking good care of me,
And that my soul has found peace within.
Know that I am collecting my broken
Pieces in a woven basket, gifted
By my mother.
No, I haven't been okay.
Know the past is resurfacing, and I don't
Know how to meet younger me and
Look into her sunken eyes.
How do I hold her frail bones next to my
Big ones with thick flesh on top, and not
Fear breaking her?

Rational Breathing

Sometimes my anxiety is rational.
Sometimes it's, "oh my God, heights!"
But
Sometimes it's, "oh my God, am I gonna let my future
Children in
10 years, go trick or treating?
What if someone sticks a razor in their candy?"
Sometimes my depression is rational.
Sometimes it's, "oh my God, the world is dying"
But
Sometimes it's, "oh my God, someone looked at me the
Wrong way,
How will I survive?"
Sometimes my paranoia is rational.
Sometimes it's "you're being followed"
But
Sometimes it's, "I'm being followed by the Italian
Mafia and they know that one time
Back in the fourth grade,
I looked at someone else's test for an answer
And now it's payback time."
Sometimes my eating disorder is rational.
Sometimes it's, "hey, maybe two cinnamon rolls is
Enough for this hour."
But
Sometimes it's, "damn, the cook at
A&W accidentally put mayo on my vegan
Beyond Meat burger, and that's because
God is telling me I'm too fat already, so I shouldn't eat it,
And the mayo is my punishment."

Whether or not my mind makes sense,
It's my mind and I love it.
I wouldn't want it to be any other way.
Sometimes, a lot of the time, I think
About killing myself. But then I think
About how I wouldn't do it right and how
Awkward that would be to explain, so I
Don't even try anymore.
No matter how irrational my thoughts are,
There's always part of me on the outside
Looking in saying, "It's okay. Breathe."
And so, I do.

My Point Always Gets Lost

The chaos in my brain is the same
Chaotic energy as when I woke up at
3AM to newly born kittens on the floor.
The chaotic part is that I didn't know my
Indoor cat
Was pregnant. But the even more odd
Part is that our other cat is a girl,
Or so we thought.
The thing is, life can be as predictable as you
Plan it, but something will always pop up
Out of the blue.
Out of the blue...

I find it funny how the reason I started
Smoking weed was because of a guy
Who had never even touched the plant, but
Broke my heart. I needed something
To ease the sorrow, so I turned to a new
Lover instead. One that was always at my
Beck and call, and never refused to love me.

However, I kept smoking because of the guys
Who did smoke, too. Now, I'm lost and
Confused and
Not sure why I even waste my money
This way. It's a headache that cannot be cured,
Unless I smoke more weed to ease the pain.
See how it gets repetitive?
I mean, God forbid I smoke a jay
After a long day.
There's nothing more numbing
Than icy cold green coasting through
My mind, on a surfboard, nonetheless.
At least it's not popping more pills, right?
That's gotta give me some leeway.

That's another thing, boy do I hate
Having to rely on medication to stop
Me from climbing up a big ol' building and
Saying farewell to the world.
How weird is it, that I literally cannot
Function without three different pills in
My system?
I mean, at least it's no longer four.
The night terrors aren't as often or
Memorable, so I gave up the sleeping pill.
Where was I going again?

Oh yea, so my cat gave birth. Damn, I
Really got off track. There's just so much
In my head.
Out of the blue.
Out of the blue...

I'm only 20! Wait, no, I'm still 19.
Shit! I'm only 19. I'm still so young.
My being is no older than the Toyota Prius.
My soul is no younger than this universe.
I've seemed to have forgotten where I
Planted my roots. I dug them up about
6 months ago and gave them a nice little
Pot to sit in. It's only a pot and not a garden,
Because I can't afford a lawn yet.

A lawn, oh my God, how I dream of owning
A lawn. I dream of building a tiny home
With the one I long to spend the rest of
My days with.
Out of the blue.
Out of the blue...

I can't tell which way the wind is blowing,
The breeze is so light it barely tosses
My pixie cut. But that doesn't stop me
From trying to fly a kite.
Flying a kite was my favourite thing to
Do with my dad as a kid.
Dad,
Why didn't you confront him, then and there?
I feel like I'm trapped inside my own nutshell,
Just waiting to be cracked open.
They say people with mental issues are unstable
And hard to love,
But I don't believe that's true.
What about me makes it hard to love me?
The constant worry for the wellbeing of
My partner? The agonizing pain from anxiety
Over who gets to cook dinner tonight?
Oh, maybe my bleeding heart makes me
Hard to love. I can imagine he's tired
Of cleaning up after me.
Out of the blue.
Out of the blue...
At least I'm eating again.
Not starving myself for someone else to
Love me, no. I'm whole again.
At least I haven't been hospitalized for over
6 Months!
That's a normal thing to be thrilled about,
Right? At least I'm not locked up between
Four piss coloured walls and
A watching eye hovering my every move.

Where was I going again?
My cats! Yes, my cats. They provide so much
Love, comfort and purpose for me. They
Make me feel like my family is complete.
They make me feel like I have a responsibility:
To keep them happy and healthy.

I know this poem has been a whole
Lot of chaos, kind of like Aries season,
But that's what my brain is like all of the goddamn
Time. No wonder I'm always exhausted.
I'm not sure any of this made sense,
As my point always gets lost within a task.
But please don't judge the mania behind this
Porcelain mask.

To Be His Lioness

I fell in love with a Leo.
Playful, romantic; the whole sun upon
His eyelids.
When we kiss, it's like tulips bloom in the
Breath of fresh spring.
When we laugh, it's like lupins awaken
From the frosting of winter.
When we love, it's like an endless meadow
Accompanies us, and doves let out a tune.

I fell in love with a Leo.
Hurt, passionate; the whole galaxy
Under his skin.
When he's down, all of the leaves fall
Off the trees.
When he's upset, every cloud turns into
A tornado and rips through the city.
When he's depressed, everyone turns into
The enemy...
Except for me.

We are two separate people from the
Same troubled soul.
In a past life, you can bet we were in love
Then too.
It took me so long to find you, but we were
Never truly apart. You were the guardian
Angel sending strength to me
When I needed you most.
You are the guardian angel keeping me safe
Everyday, wherever I go.

You are the Dragonball to my Z,
The oat milk to my cookie,
The apple of my eye,
The low to my high.
You are the father to my future children;
The person I will grow old with if I am lucky.
You are the gravitational pull to my orbit,
The hickory to my dickory doc.
You are all I've ever needed, wanted, craved.
You are all I'll ever need, want, and crave.
You are my heart's only desire.

I fell in love with a Leo.
He is brave, he is charming, he is powerful.
He is everything I could have, and did, ask for.

The Attic

Looking at you while doing the dishes,
Towel draped around your shoulder,
Focus perched upon your expression;
I had this sudden, overwhelming sensation
Of love for you.
You really have been trying your best,
And my God, do I appreciate it.

For a second there, I thought I lost my
Inspiration, so I glanced at your face and
Oh! There it is again.

Our apartment is a fucking disaster,
But it's still where we rest our heads
Together at night.
This is still our breakfast date spot,
Our battleground,
Our safe space,
Our place.
No, it may not be too homelike
To the eye,
But that's because it's not.

There are leaks in the ceiling,
Cracks in the doors,
Broken locks,
Crooked cupboards, and
Dirty windows too far from my reach.
But none of that matters to me.
These are still the four walls that hear
Our secret '*I love you*'s,

And our good morning slogans.
This is still the place that I get to spend all
Of my rest time with the love of my life.
It is what we can afford,
It is where our rescued kitties play all day.
Here is where we love.
Here is where we are.
So let's make the most out of this third floor
Loft.
For it is ours.
Ours.

Tuesdays at 5

I wish I could tell you something positive.
I wish I could lie and say it's okay.
But this world is a shithole and
The people in it are making it that way.

She tells me she's proud of me,
Which are words I've craved hearing
For years now.
But maybe I've been lying to her,
Maybe that's why she thinks so highly of me.
The thing is, a therapist
Can't be your friend, but to me,
She is. How could she not be?
She saved my life many times.
But now our time together is
Ending, and
Our sessions are cut short by loss
Of words.
I've grown- she
Has watered my roots and watched
Me flourish.

Who will help me grow now that
I'm alone again? Do I wait for
It to rain? Do I plop myself down in
The bathtub and let the shower
Head soak me? That could be dangerous
As the soaking would kill my roots.
Fuck, why are even essential things
Capable of killing us?
It's like everything is out to get me;
One thing after another.
Domino's falling one by one.

Breathe. She'd tell me to breathe.
Then, she'd laugh and say "check the facts-"
Laughing because I know
It's the next step.

The world is a horrible place-
No, the world has bad things happening,
But there is still beauty among the
Chaos.
Everything is filled with pain-
No, grief will come like waves
And when the tide goes out again,
All of the pain will flood away too.
People want to hurt me-
The people in my circle have good
Intentions, and if I find out they don't,
Then I'll show them the door.

Tuesdays at 5, for the rest of my life,
Will be dedicated to my healing.
This poem is dedicated to her.

These words aren't coming out right,
I want to write you the most beautiful
Poem you've ever read, because that's
What you deserve. But the words
Just aren't flowing, the emotions are.
There I go again, emotion mind
Over wise mind.

You created a safe space for me to vent,
For me to show my traumas in full
Colour, and sort through my tangled
Ball of yarn.
You stitched my sleeve so the heart
Stays put,
And didn't even shudder at the
Crooked tales I'd speak.
There's no simple way to put it:
The reason I'm still alive is you.

The world is a shithole,
But people like you make it all worthwhile.

Cat Mum

For as long as I can remember,
I've wanted a cat.
For as long as I've loved him,
I've had two rescue kitties to call our own.
I'm a hopeless romantic,
Which makes me panic
Because there's uncertainty that circles
In my stomach, churning for hours on end.
Uncertainty from where I am going in life.
Where have I even left?
You see, I live in a dump.
I've been abused and used and thrown out
Like trash- believe me, I'm over it.
I left a job I barely even had-
Yes, yes, it was for my own sanity, I know.
What have I got? What am I? Who am I?
These questions tumble and scurry into
Hidden corners in my blacked out mind.
Blacked out by memory loss
Triggered by no fault of my own.
Triggered by trauma I thought only happened
In fiction.
This was supposed to be a poem about
My fucking cats,
Not the monster that still lives under my bed.
I thought the nightlight would help me
Be not so scared at night, but I guess
All I needed was his arms.

I guess all I need is to slow down and rethink
My shapeshifting blessings; the ones that
Look like curses but are actually lessons.
I had a friend tell me that life is all about lessons,
And the world is my school. We don't naturally die until
All of our lessons are learned, or else we come back.
And hell, I don't want to come back.
So I'm here to live and learn as much as
I can.
Lesson of the day: count your blessings.
My blessings are here at home.

Sweet 16

Sliced wrists under sweaters
And a glowing smile-
Everything looked...okay?
Baggy clothes protecting my frail
Image.
One boy dared to ask me if
My old, tight clothes just didn't fit anymore-
To which I couldn't think of a proper response.
That's the thing with me;
Any time someone offends me, I tend to
Freeze up and choke.
Choking, choked,
Choke- he would choke me.
He would bury me beneath the snow
Of the Swiss Alps, if he could.
He would hold me down,
He would push my face away.
He would go until all that was happening,
Was pain.
But still I "forget" all that because I'm
"Healing," I'm a "survivor."
I forget all of these things he would do
Until I walked into his favourite store today and
Checked every nook and cranny
In case I saw his face.

His eyes,
The memory of his eyes
Scares the absolute hell out of me.
So dark,
So miserable.
Marble beads, some may say.

I've been finding you less and less
In this world, but boy do I still
Fear the day we spot one another unexpectedly.
Sure, I should be over it by now. It's
Been a year!
But the thing is, it has only been
A year since I started to heal from the
Damage you put me in for two years and
Counting.
I hate your guts.
I wish you poorly, and if that means poor
Happens me, so be it.
I did not deserve what you did to me.

Why the fuck am I still writing about
16 year old me?
I have a lover that runs to our shared
Bedroom and tells me I am loved, valued
And appreciated, just totally out of the blue!
He loves me unconditionally,
To the point where I don't think of why
He shouldn't love me.

He doesn't get mad that I'm still stuck
In a 16 year old's body and mindset.
He doesn't mind that I'm still healing,
Still figuring out where all of my missing
Pieces are.
Hell, he doesn't even question it when
My broken porcelain cuts his fingertips
As they run down my frame.
He is the beacon of light at the end of a tunnel.

My Sweet 16 may not have been so sweet.
But maybe the next few years to come will be
With him by my side.

Duck Tube Socks

Two days ago, I was in the ER
Because I wanted to kill myself.
I still want to, but now I'm out and walking
Around this earth like nobody can see the
Furrow of my eyebrows as I plot a plan.
But no, I never "have a plan,"
And I guess that's a good thing.

The crisis nurse asked me what keeps
Me from ending it.
My answer wasn't what she had hoped.
She had hoped I'd say the love from my
Fiancé, my interests and hobbies,
My family, but no.
I said the only reason I don't is because
I probably wouldn't do it right and
I'd be left having to explain myself.

Lupins and ocean spray are what I miss.
Fields of green and yellow bliss.
Dandelions below my shoes.
Delicate sky blue and grey hues.

I kept looking at my feet;
Yellow stained tennis shoes and
My sister's duck tube socks.
I cry at the innocents I've lost, or
Never really had.
I shy away from the innocents I still have,
And unlock the door to the ground below.

Locked. The door is locked.
The sky is still blue and grey but
I cannot see it.
Dandelions and lupins still bloom.
My tennis shoes are still yellow and
Still have my feet occupying their space.

I'm tired of writing about the same shit.
The same abuse they don't believe, or
Would rather see run away from me.
I'm tired of fighting so damn hard
Every day, just to get two steps ahead,
Then three steps back.

Today, I am 20 years old.
I am the youngest I'll ever be again.
But I still hold on to the pain,
For it is all I've ever known
And the pain of letting go is too much
To bare for a fragile heart.

To The Boy Who Can't Even Butter His Own Toast

Every night, more and more, I lay on
"Your side" of the bed.
But not because I miss you,
Long for your embrace; no.
It's because I'm taking back
My whole bed.
Every day, less and less, I think about you.
But it's not because I miss you,
Long for your embrace; no.
It's because I'm taking back my thoughts.

I spent two or more months debating if it was
My fault. If the sexual abuse was
Because I didn't say no.
If the being used and
Belittling was because my voice was too
Shaky to fight against it. If putting in all the
Effort myself was the only reason we were
Together.

I'm tired of sitting and stirring in my own
Shit because of you. I'm tired of hurting
Over the memories and the flashbacks
And the constant fear that I'll see you
Somewhere. I'm tired of
Thinking I'm to blame for everything-
Like I'm the reason you stopped loving me.

But hell, if that's the case, I'm the
Reason you never started loving me.
But I'm also the reason your mom
Had a second daughter. I'm the
Reason you had your first kiss.
I'm the reason you smiled as often
As you did. Fuck it, I hope I'm the reason
You're sad.

I hope your soul realized
That your happiness stopped being
My 11:11 wish.
I hope your cat misses me more than
He misses you when you stay away
At your dads.
I hope that porn becomes your only
Friend.
I hope that sadness becomes your middle name.

But I don't actually, do I?
Of course not, because I'm too sweet.
In reality, I hope you love someone
Just as much as I loved you.
And I hope more than anything,

That they break your heart the same
Way you broke mine.

The R Word

I don't know what's going on inside.
One minute I'm numb, the next I feel everything.
Anything.
It's like I'm in grade 8 math class all over again,
Because nothing makes sense.
I'm terrified of everything.
I'm terrified of getting out of bed, but I'm
Terrified to be in bed because that bed is
The one that holds all of the bad memories.
Maybe all I need to do is buy a new bed...
If I had the money.
Huh, I'm sleeping in the bed I was raped in
Just because I don't have enough money
To buy a new one.
It's not a big deal I suppose, it's not even like
I can call it rape anyway.
Why does that word scare everyone so much?
It happens, so don't act like it doesn't.
Allow us to say the R word to describe
What happened to us.
Allow us to freely speak of our fellow
Survivors
And use the word then too.
Don't sugarcoat it,
Don't butter it up to be something else
When it's not.

But even after saying that,
The word still scares me.
It scares me because I feel like I can't
Use it to describe what happened to me.
It's like my experience isn't valid because
I didn't say no, he was my boyfriend, not
Some stranger in an alley. Our perception
Of what can be classified as rape is so
Fucked up. Any sexual act that isn't
Wanted by another, should be called rape.
But I guess you have to consider what they
Were wearing, if they were sober, or if they
Even said no, right?
I just wish the signs of trauma were
Enough to be believed.
The nightmares where I physically kick you off
Me. The mental breakdowns because
I remember more details.
Wanting to shower for a second
Time today because of how dirty I feel.
Dirty. I feel dirty. I feel used and abused
And filthy. I feel filthy.
My body doesn't feel like it belongs to me.
I lost that privilege at 16.
I'm so tired of thinking about this.
I just want a hug, but I don't
Want to be trapped.
Maybe I'll just start to save up more to buy
A new bed and hope that sorts out
My issues.

Silence is Wishful Thinking

I wish you could kiss my mind
To shut up my thoughts.

Metal Spoons

Trembling tones in response to
Wicked questions about life or death.
The ER has never been so familiar.
I spent 5 days there when I was 16,
And I promised myself no more.

A night by my dad's side,
Safe yet in complete darkness.
Begging for some relief,
Which just happened to be Ativan.

Drop. I drop off to sleep.
The day does not leave me behind,
As I stir in these sheets.

I'm thankful for a safe night's rest.
I'm thankful to have passed God's test.

"You did the right thing by calling me,"
Says dad. I cry because I wasn't sure.
I don't mean to be a bother, I'm just a lost
Soul looking for shallow water.
But for now, I'll spread this jam
On my toast with a metal spoon.
And maybe this time,
The ER was worth the wait.

Let's Talk About the Psych Ward

Involuntarily placed in a psych ward, is a
Brilliant way to start off your 20's.
Locked in the back of an ambulance for a
50 minute drive, with no idea what road I'm on,
Which makes me even more panicked.
At least they let me have my phone back. I texted
Friends and family
Like my fingers were on fire and the keys
Would put the flames out.
I don't utter a word until the paramedic
Starts asking me questions. Questions
That you'd ask some randomly sane person
Next to you in line at a coffee shop.
I answer as short and sweet as possible.
My mind is just running nonstop, and I
Can't keep up with his friendliness.

Once we get to the unit,
I take in my last few breaths of fresh air for a week.
I memorize the other side of the door that
Will lock me in here for far too long.

My things get searched, money gets counted,
Pills get tucked away somewhere safe, and
I get tucked away somewhere safe.

A room with a number I don't memorize
Because I never look at it twice, in fear
That those
Three numbers will follow me forever.
And now I'm thinking, 605. Now I'm thinking
Are these the numbers?
Are these the numbers?
Are these the three or has my brain just
Accumulated another memory, like,
This is just a number, here's a number to
Cling to.
I always find something to cling to.

I was always unhappy as a kid. I never
Felt right. What happened to me that made
Me feel like my body wasn't my body, like
My voice wasn't my voice,
Like my "no's" came out as nothing,
Like my tears at a sleepover at night was
Me fearing someone would violate me,
Like why did I miss mummy and daddy
So much,
Like why do I still fear touches,
Kisses, hugs, pats on the back?
Tell me what the fuck happened that makes me
Shake because I can't quite remember
Yesterday, let alone life before
9, other than what I'm told.
I know we moved,
I've always known that alone was traumatic
For me.

I'm snapped back into the world as
The paramedic pulls me aside in my
Gently interesting room: mushy green coloured
Walls, a bed, a window the size of my
Hopes and dreams,
But guess what, those
Are locked too.

"You don't belong in here" he says.
My eyes well up even more.
The door has no doorknob, I quickly assess.
The look in his eyes was enough to tell
Me he believed his own words on my
Behalf.
A thank you slips out of my butchered lips,
And he leaves the room.

I'm given about five minutes to have the
Biggest breakdown of my life.
Like holy fuck, how did I end up

In a psych ward.... involuntarily?
I can't even blame my paranoia, because
That has settled down a bit, right?

But seriously, what the hell happened
Me, that locked me up in here?
What was the trigger,
The first domino tipping over,
The first "oh, shit" moment?

I cannot, for the life of me, remember.
So if you know why, please tell me.

Regret

The weird part of this whole thing is
That I feel like
I've been here before.

My head's spinning,
Back's aching,
Tummy's churning.

Not even when I
Go to sleep, am I escaping
This place. It's in my dreams.

I wake up startled,
So scared,
So panicked.

I wish I could take
Back that phone call,
And just breathe instead.
Maybe then, I'd be safe at home.

Nightmares From Another Realm

God only knows what time it is right now.
Vision blurred, words and letters
Collide. The only noise is my
Pen against this paper, and a
Low hum coming from above.
I'm tired, but unable to sleep.
The nightmares wake me up
In cold sweats.
I miss him. I miss my babies.
I miss driving and singing. I miss work.
I miss feeling like a human, or at least
Myself. My only company
Is the moon,
And she's alone too.
She has always been there
When I needed her most,
Now, more than ever.

Engagement Nails

My engagement nails
Look an awful lot different
Than my hospital nails.
All of the gems were either
Picked off from anxiety
Or fell off from wear.
My thumb nail is broken,
And all of them have outgrown themselves.
I'll be embarrassed when I go
To get them done again,
But boy, oh boy,
I hope that's soon.

Failing Mindfulness

Wisdom.
What does that even mean?
All I can think of is my niece bouncing on
My sister's knee.
Wisdom.
 "Wise men say it's better to have a good day,"
Is the response I get from another patient,
When asking
How he's doing. He says,
"It's even better because it all rhymes."
Wisdom. Let the cars and people pass by.
But when I do that,
All I can do is sigh.
I wonder why, but I soon realize.
It's no fun watching other people be happy,
When all you want to do is die.

All of These Are Written In Marker

Sleepless nights.
Not quite forgetting,
But not quite remembering
What it's like to fall asleep in his arms.
Total security in his embrace.
He cuddles my sweater instead.
I sleep beside a picture of him
Next to my head.
Lump in my throat
As I write these words.
Maybe we're asleep together in another world.

Patience

Being a patient is a waiting game.
I guess that's why they call it patience.
Waiting all weekend for a doctor,
Waiting all night for morning.
Patience. I was never good at waiting.
Whether that be for Christmas presents,
My own engagement, or for things to get better.
Radical acceptance at its prime is
Accepting that I'll be here for a while.
First, I accept that I won't get out of going to the unit.
Secondly, I had to accept that I wouldn't be leaving
All weekend.
Then, I had to accept that I just might not see
Him every day.
Patience. It's an awful lesson to learn when there's
Nothing else to do.

A Wishful Goodnight

Butterflies flutter the first time
We met, kissed, laughed, loved.
Butterflies flutter now 9 months later,
At the thought of coming home to you.
I daydream over feeling your
Hand on my thigh, as I drive
Down a back road, on our way to the
Gardens of Hope.
The memory fades, the longer I am trapped inside
These four walls.
But butterflies still flutter when I close my eyes at night
And imagine your lips pressing a kiss to my forehead,
With well wishes.

Recreate

I am blessed for the reason
My skin sheds.
My skin has lost every inch you ever betrayed.
My skin has renewed itself with
Flowers, butterflies, a whole damn garden.
My skin has regained my DNA, and only mine.
No more toxins, no more bruises attached
To my frail self.
No more need to shudder at my own reflection,
As I washed your touch down the drain.
I scrubbed myself clean. But you,
You are forever dirty, for you
Are the one who has sinned.

Home At Last

It's strange being home again.
When the car pulled up to my house,
I felt like an alien landing it's spaceship
In unfamiliar territory.
The memories soon zapped back into my
Brain, as quickly as those sleeping
Pills knocked me out in there.
My God, how relieving it was to walk
In the front porch and smell home for
The very first time.
Home smells like a freshly opened
Book, ocean spray candles, and a
Little bit of kush.
Home looks like golden picture frames,
A full but clean dishwasher, and sounds
Like a tumbling laundry machine.
Home tastes like bruschetta, humidity,
And his lips.
It's a smell, view, and taste I never want
To forget or be apart from ever again.

Rose Bush

Being a mental patient is like
Stripping naked in a room full of thorns.
Exposed and hurt in a crowded room.
I've never had more power than telling
Him to leave the unit, though it was
The last thing I really wanted.
Sweet guitar riffs, and melodies too
True to a mind in pain.
Words were my first love, and they
Shall be my last, with my lover by my side
Whispering, "Welcome home."

Karma's A Bitch, & So Are You

Anytime I unbuckle my belt,
I feel your hands prying it open-
And gripping at my hips to take off my
Jeans, as I squirm in my place.
Sometimes, I want this.
Sometimes, you push my face away
So you don't have to look at my
Tears. That disgusts me,
And yet I lay there like a doll:
Like an object for you to crawl inside of.
Anytime my legs are even slightly apart,
I feel your invasion among them-
And gripping at my hips to take control,
As I freeze in this place.
I had spluttered the words "I forgive you"
Out of my chapped lips,
But I don't.
Instead, I forgive myself for letting my self
Worth be deemed so low. I forgive myself
For not walking away, and for walking back
After you locked me out.
I do not forgive you.
And I sure hope that your gift of pain
Is en route to your doorstep.

Seamless

It's 3AM and I just smoked a bowl of
My very good frenemy.
I love her, but she's not good
For me.
She eases the pain; takes it away completely
At times.
When we're mixed together,
It's like water and wine-
Seamless.
But sometimes she's too much.
She can make me feel like my knees
Have given out, and like domino's,
Everything else comes next.
My poor lungs; my poor, poor lungs.
She's not good for my bank account
Either. She drains it dry
Like a puddle in mid-August.
But I suppose I could use the money
On worse friends. Friends who don't
Pay me back with companionship.
First of all, she never bails when we
Want to hang out:
And she never judges me for sleeping when
We do.
She makes me laugh, like, a lot
And reassures me that everything will
Be okay.

But sometimes she's the reason
I don't see that anything is okay.
Sometimes she's the negative force
Dragging me down, and spitting me out
Half chewed.
I know our friendship is unhealthy, but
God, would I miss her presence if I chose
To leave her.
Her sweet aroma carries through the air
And I choke up. Not because of the smoke,
But because I know I will have to give
Her up some day.
And hell, maybe that day should be
Sooner than today, but it's going
To take a big force to change
My habit.

Counting Sheep

The history of my luck isn't too
Great, I'm surprised you didn't turn
Up without a pulse.
After all of those days of searching high and low,
How did you survive the darkness
You faced alone?
I wish I could've ran away and found you
On those sleepless nights,
Instead of counting sheep.
I carried the weight of waiting for you
For so long, I'm still holding on in fear that
If I let go, you'd slip through my fingers.
How was I to know you were 45 minutes
Away in the other direction?
Now that I've got you, how will I ever
Let you go?
When the time is here, how will I say
Goodbye? I find it hard enough to stay asleep
Because I miss you too much, and I wake up
And just stare at every inch of your face until
I find a new detail I never noticed before.
With that said, I fall in love all over again.

So my love, promise me
A home built from love, and
A garden sprouting heavenly hues of
Greenery and infinite possibilities.
Promise me the children I have carried
Half of, for my whole life.
Promise me good morning kisses, and
Outdated arguments that lead to more
Kisses.
Promise me old age and laughter.

Promise me that we will never bore each
Other.

Take me back to the night I first laid
Eyes on you. Take me back to the first
Smile we exchanged, and first kiss I dodged,
So I can go back and kiss you.
Take me back so I can hold you tighter
Than the first hug I gave you.
I would tell you all of the secrets I
Know now, about how quickly we'd
Fall in love and how at home we would
Feel soon.
I wish I could have found you sooner and
Prevented all of the hurt from ever crossing
Your path. But I guess we both had to learn
A lot before we could ever love each other.

Growing Into Myself

We all have different phases throughout
Our lives on who we are.
We are not the same person we were at 16,
Than we are at 35.
I am not the same person I was before I met
You, nor will I stay the same person I was
The night that we met.
I have changed since then; flourished beyond
Measures I thought I was capable of.
I'm okay with living now: that's a big thing
For me. I'm okay with going to sleep and
Waking up for another day again because
I'm living another day with you.
I'm okay with going to work, because I get to
Miss you and then come home to you
And feel so relieved that you're in my
Arms again.

Speaking of going to work, damn do I hate
It because you're not around. But boy do
I love it when you surprise me and enter
The restaurant for supper, or a grab and go
Lemonade.

Boy do I love that we have a family together:
Just us and the three cats.
I love how you love me with dandelion
Bouquets, or a packed
Pipe waiting for me on the table.
I love how you hold me so securely, but
Not trapping me. I love how you
Don't stutter to say "I love you,"
Or "you're the love of my life."
Hell, I know you're the love of my life,
But I still stutter to say it because I'm scared.
I'm scared that those words will come back to
Bite me in the ass, because they have before.
But that doesn't mean this is the same.
As I said, I'm not the same person I was
At 16, nor will I be the same at 35,
But I know for a fact my love for you will forever
Stay the same. I know that, because love
Is timeless. Love grows. Love flourishes.
Love blooms. Love talks in a mellow voice
Instead of angry when they're upset. I'm sorry
I get upset.

It's like 10,000 knives are stuck in my back
All at once and someone screws them
Around a bit, just for fun.
I get angry because I'm angry at a lot of things
That I let slide.
I'm angry about how I've been treated by others.
I'm angry about how others treat others.
I'm angry for 16 year old me,

But do you know what? I'm manifesting
For 35 year old me. I'm manifesting being
Your wife, and living within motherhood.
I'm manifesting growth together.
I'm manifesting a life described in fairytales;
Ones that we will tell to our children.

I cannot wait for life with you.
I cannot wait to meet the next phase of you.
As I grow into myself once again, please
Intertwine with me a little bit more as you
Grow up too.

Dear Mother, I'm Sorry

The trees you planted and watered from a seed
That grew into mighty barks of life,
Are being murdered by the men that took
Their breath away.

The oceans that provided homes for your angelic
Sea creatures, has turned into their own personal
Hell, as pure rubbish has crammed their
Space so much that it's wrapped around their necks.

I think about you all of the time and I hear your
Cries for help. I hear them in the storms you
Make and the
Countless forests burnt to a crisp. I hear them
In the corners of the streets that are polluted
By the engines of our motors for drive,
But we seem to stall when you cross the street.

I'm not sure, Mother, how to come home to you
For a home cooked meal and stare right
Into your eyes as I take a bite of your precious gift,
After you have slaved over a solar oven all day.

Where can I go, Mother, where I no longer
Am reminded of your tortured soul
Or your crumbling surface, without feeling
Guilty for wanting peace of mind?

I am ashamed that my brothers and sisters do
Not have the same urge to fight for your
Well-being; or maybe they have been
Too sheltered and haven't experienced the trauma.

Mother, why did you let us get so out of
Control? Mother, why did I just put the blame
On you? Mother, please tuck me in tonight
With your loving grace and sing a lullaby to ease
This headache.

I complain about my head that is spinning, but
At least it is spinning. Soon this Earth won't-
And I don't want to bury you. So please, just
Don't die on me.

I'm sorry that we took advantage of you.
I'm sorry that you're dying and that we are killing you.
I'm sorry, I'm sorry, I'm sorry.
Please forgive us.

Survivor

I explain too much when I talk, but
Even when I write. So let me try to cut
It down...

Videotaped memories
Are all I have,
Floating between the shelves in
My parents basement,
Or countless frozen images saved on phones.

That's still too many words.

Pears. Dad and I would pick pears
Off the tree in the yard.

Yard. There's a picture of me asleep
In our brickyard when I was little.

Picture. How I try to capture so much
In one image.

Still, there are too many words.
Silent. I should be silent.

Should. I should be nothing but what they
Expect of me.

Expectations. You had always let me down.

I'm always let down.

Not enough words. I'm not using enough
Words. I bet that's what he'll say.
He'll tell me I didn't use my words like the
Big girl I am. He'll say I didn't say no.

How can someone push anothers face
Away and pretend it's okay, and keep
Forcing their presence inside until
It hurts so bad they want to die?

Tetris. Tetris on my TV screen
And another memory is unlocked.
You taught me how to play Tetris
And I became better than you... almost.
These are the memories that come back
That confuse the hell out of me.
How could someone be so two faced?
So split? How did we go from sweet kissing,
To you going longer than anticipated
Or desired.
How did it go from "when we get married"
To "I don't think we're right for each other"?

But boy, oh boy, am I sure glad it went that way.
I couldn't imagine living under
Your spell for a lifetime.
Instead, I am under the care and tenderness
Of another.
I am protected by a safe haven and kitten
Fur.
I was rescued from a burning house and
Was whisked away like a sack of spuds.

I still have moments where I'm laying on
The edge of my bed and I have to tell myself,
"Nobody is going to undress you and
Hold you down."
I still have to tell myself that when my
Lover is tickling me, that he won't do anything
But tickle me.

I'm so furious that you took my
Innocents and boiled it under high heat,
Until it turned sour.
I'm so angry that I didn't wake up until
You had cut me loose.
I'm so mad because I still haven't
Confronted you about everything.
God knows if you've done this to other people
By now...
But that's not my fault. That's not my problem.
You are not my problem.

My problems consist of making sure my family
Is okay, and I am sane enough to go to work.
My problems no longer intersect with
Aggression meeting fear.

I am not what you did to me.
I am who I am because I survived.

Discrete

Happiness is like the moment I drop off to sleep.
It's rare, hard to notice, until I start dreaming.

Realization

I've been feeling
Less depressed, I think.
I say "I think" because there's
A possibility I'm just becoming
Used to it or going numb.
But my thoughts haven't been so loud,
And my words have been a little kinder.
Maybe the sky is brighter,
Or maybe my eyes are just sensitive
From being closed away in the dark all of the time.

Let's be real, I don't
Really want to die,
I don't think anyone really does,
I just want the pain to stop.
I don't even want to
Write about my lack of will
To live.
I'd rather write about the
Glistening in his eyes
When he looks at me,
And how quickly it turns into
A flame.
I'd rather give power to
The goosebumps I get
Throughout my entire body when
He touches me,
Kisses me,
Loves on me.

The thing is, I don't know where I'm going.
But I know he'll follow close behind
Wherever it is I decide to go.
The truth is, his soul is the purest
I've ever known. Someone so honestly
Trying. So persistent in getting better.

I'm in love with him,
I truly am.
The reason I'm not feeling so depressed,
Is him.

A Million Times

Last night,
You broke up with me a million times.
It was all in my head, but
Boy, oh boy, did I
Expect those words to leave your mouth
And break my heart.

They never did though.
Those words,
My thoughts
Were more powerful
Than any paranoia
I've faced before;
And I used to hear voices.

But instead of leaving me in the dust,
You stripped my soul naked.
You cleaned my aura of
Deep purple bruises and scars I've become
Such good friends with,
They have names.

I stumble over possibilities
Of why you didn't just
Give up on me,
Right then and there.
The two reasons I end up with are
Because you'd be lonely without me,
And just maybe,
You truly love me.
My bet is on the latter.

I promise I'm trying.

Pinky swear with spit
On my thumb,
I'm going to get better.
Please don't forget the real me
When my demons take over.

Perceptive Wisdom

If I were to list the things that
Confuse me, I'd run out of ink.
I'd be better to list
What I find understandable.

I understand that not everyone is
Dealt an easy deck.
I understand that in order to
Boil water, the kettle must be hot.
I understand why a walk in the park
Is a luxury, and it's one I no longer take
For granted.
I understand that feeling weak
And feeling strong is all in how we
Perceive it ourselves.
I may not know an awful lot,
But I can soothe a crying child with a hug.
I use my car signals in roundabouts,
Because otherwise, accidents happen.
I know how to link words together
To provoke emotions deep within.

I may not understand
Math, science, or what it means to be
Mentally well,
But I have years of wisdom beyond my time.

Depression Snack

I yell out to you that I've also been irritated
By my weight today and I'm having a
Depression snack to ease the pain,
And you yell back that I'm beautiful.

Takis are my depression snack today.
I guess they're my punishment.
First of all, they're spicy as fuck.
Secondly, they make me feel numb when
I eat them.
Thirdly, it brings me back to a time I'd much
Rather forget.

I think the reason I'm eating them is just
So I feel worse about everything, as dumb
As that may sound.
The flashbacks I get are colored with a tint
Of grey, and green.

I was sitting in the hallway next to my old
Locker in high school.
Thigh gap between my legs, and an
Oblivious state of mind as to what
Happens in the next few months.

The part I'm not trying to think about
Was my company when I was eating
Those Takis for the first time.

I usually don't remember things, but
I can remember this day clear as mud.
I thought it was a good day.

We walked to the closest convenience
Store and bought lemonades, airheads,
And Takis.
I hate that I just said
We.

You're a whole other person since then,
And so am I.
A person I'd rather not think about
When I see a red Pontiac on the highway.
A person I'd rather not get triggered by
When your name is brought up
In conversation.

Everyone knows, but nobody knows,
What you did to me.
And maybe that's okay. Maybe they
Don't need to know the whole truth.
They just need to know you did wrong.

I'm not sorry I'm not quiet about your wrongs.
I'm not even sorry I messaged your mum;
A breath of fresh air, that was.
I'm not sorry for seeing a person you weren't,
And for loving him fully.
I'm not sorry for being upset over this either.

Yea, time heals all wounds, but some
Wounds leave scars.
But don't be sorry for me,
I'll get a pretty tattoo over the scars so
I only see beauty, and not the pain
You left me alone to deal with.

Skint

Spending all of my time
Loving you,
Let's hope I don't go broke.

Holding on like you're a life raft,
But my thoughts
Won't stay afloat.

I worry that when life
Becomes sweet,
I'll become diabetic.

What I mean by that, is
That things tend to turn sour when they're
Good for a while.

It's almost like there's a happiness meter
And when I reach the max,
It breaks because there's too much to contain.

So then I fall down like a sack of spuds,
Since there's nowhere left to remain.

But I'll find it all again,
As soon as I spend all of my time
Loving you

I Do

Ever since I was born,
I hated change. Birth itself was
So abstract to me, I couldn't breathe.

I remember graduating from grade 6
And crying at the end of the ceremony.
My friend had tried comforting me,
And I often look back on what had
Upset me so much.

I've come to the conclusion that
I hate change, and I knew deep down
That everything was going to change
Again in middle school.

Middle school was tough as nails
For me. It's when I really
Started thinking about killing myself.
It's when the bullying really kicked in.
It's when the food restrictions began.

Now I look back and feel so sad
For younger me.
I feel so sorry for the nights she
Had to hold herself while crying.
I feel so sorry for the cuts she drew
Upon her wrists and legs, that carried
On for years to come.
I feel so sorry for the childhood carelessness
That she lost due to mental illness.

I have learned how to
Manage things other people only
Witness in horror films, and
I make it look like a slightly twisted fairytale.

I flip like a switch-
Go out like a light,
And then everything is dark.
Today, I wanted everything to go dark.
Today, I wanted nothing at all, but
Everything all at once.
I wanted death to wash over me like
Showers from grey clouds.
But I surpassed all of those negative
Emotions and realized I'm currently
Living the dream I once created in my head
As a young one.
I am loved unconditionally,
Every single day.
I no longer have to hold myself while I cry.
I wake up to a smile on his face
Instead of being greeted
By the dread of another day.

There was a time when I was a kid,
That every morning I had awoken,
I would cry.
I would cry because I had hoped I would
Pass away in my sleep.
But no, I woke up again.
But because I woke up all of those days,
I got to meet and fall in love with
The absolute love of my life.
I get to fall in love with my curvy frame
As he compliments it for the millionth time
Today.
I get to string more words together to convey
Emotions within strangers that didn't
Even realize they had those emotions to strike.
I get to raise a furry family of three.
I get to feel the sunshine on
My youthful skin.

Without the struggles I face,
I wouldn't be me.
I wouldn't care for others the way
I do.
I wouldn't feel as much as
I do.
I wouldn't think as much as
I do.

I do.
That's what we'll say some day.
That's what I never thought I'd
Be blessed enough to say.
I never thought I'd make it to 18,
Let alone my wedding day.
But this is change I am okay with.

Sticky Notes: The Continuum

My love for sticky notes
Comes from my old therapist.
She had written them after
Every single session for almost 3 years.
I kept them all.
They were a sign of
Love, care, and honest compassion.
Now that we no longer meet weekly,
I often read over the sticky notes she gave me.
The last one she had written,
She told me to continue to spread the kindness.
So I took her words with me and I
Placed sticky notes all over town.
I had handed one personally to a lady
Struggling with homelessness,
And I had later met her again outside of
My workplace.
I reminded her of the sticky note and she
Said she passed the kindness on to
Another person.

One night as I was fast asleep,
My fiancé left sticky notes all throughout
Our home, for me to find the next morning.
Then, I did the same for him after his
Performance one evening.

My old therapist came to my workplace
And ordered some food to go.
I left a sticky note on her order.
The light in her eyes was glowing,
As she said she will put the note on her mirror,
Just as I had done with all of her notes.

One act of kindness leads to another;
Remember that.

Naming The Dead

Guided meditations used to give me
Peaceful rests, but last night, it gave me
Power. Last night, I looked him dead in
The eyes and called him what he is.
I did this in front of an entire classroom.
I did this with a pixie cut and a coat
Of armour.
I did this with flames spewing from my
Honest mouth.
I did this with intention, humiliation, and
Grief in mind.
Of course he denied the truths I spoke,
And left no room for an apology, but that's
Okay. I don't want crocodile tears or a simple
Sorry. All I want is the weight off my shoulders.
When I called you a rapist, it felt like
Naming the dead. Like I was collecting
Your memory and placing your title upon
A stone.
May you rot away in yesterday,
So I can have a better tomorrow.

When Nobody Answers

When nobody picks up the phone,
My ears start ringing along with the
Dial.
I begin to panic even more, and call
Again multiple times.
When nobody picks up the phone,
I realize how much I lack in skills.
My breathing is hitched, staggered and
Failing. My blood pressure boils and
Overflows until my skin is scalding.
When nobody picks up the phone,
I question how I'll end it.
I think that maybe the reason hell has
Broke loose is because he stopped praying
For me every night.
When nobody picks up the phone, I hear
My doctor saying "everyone is anxious,
Everyone is depressed," and I feel like my
Emotions are invalid and wrong to even process.
Maybe nobody wanted to pick up,
Or maybe they're just too busy soaking up
The sun, or fixing what wasn't even broken
To begin with,
But I'll try to call again.
Just in hopes that
Someone, somewhere, will answer.

Warning Label

It's not my responsibility
To clear your name of filth.
It's not my responsibility to save your next
Victim.
It's not my responsibility to stay awake
At night wondering if you're seeking help.

My responsibility is healing the wounds
You inflicted upon me.
My responsibility is to keep my voice
Loud and boisterous when I respect
My boundaries.
My responsibility is to keep your name
Out of my mouth.

I'm tired of fighting you and getting no hits
In because, shocker, you didn't turn up
For the fight. You're too cowardly to even
Protect yourself.

The last time I saw you, I opened my arms
Wide and held onto you like you were
The saving grace I needed.
You told me then and there that you were
Expecting me to slap you in the face.
That tells me you know exactly the hell
You raised within me.
You know the abandonment issues you
Correlated between me and love.
You know the suffering and failure of will
To live you placed upon my mind.
You know the actions you took were unclean,
Unimaginative, and just plain wrong.

I found your Instagram account and noticed
That we have mutual followers.
Let's just say I unfollowed their ignorant
Asses, because I know they've read these
Poems and figured out who they're about,
But choose to follow you anyway.
Fuck, I don't want to cry over you anymore.
I want the taste of your bitterness out
Of my mouth and replace it with life's
Sweetest sugars.
I want to heal these open gashes, but
I'm not skilled enough to sew them up.
It goes unnoticed, all of the battles I fight
Daily. It goes unnoticed that you are the biggest
Problem I have, nearly two years later.

You are the reason I fear myself.
You are the reason I fear others.
I loved you so purely, so fiercely,
Without realizing it would ruin me.
I wish you came with a warning label.
That way, I would've known exactly what I
Shouldn't have signed up for.

One Week Later

I would've been buried by now.
Flowers would have rested upon my grave
And tears would've been shed to mourn
The loss of my presence.
I would've been dead by now.
Over a week ago, I wanted to end my life.
My parents would've lost a child,
My siblings, losing a sister.
My fiancé would've lost the love of his
Life, and my cats losing their mother.
My jobs would've lost a staff member,
And the streets would lose my shoes.
This is the guilt trip I play every time I
Feel the blues.

Even If You Walk Away

I'm not done loving you,
So don't give up on me.

I won't be done loving you,
Even after my lungs give up on me.

I dream of us as old folk,
Laughing until dawn like the old days.

I dream of us on the sea at sunset,
And blissful smiles upon our faces.

I picture us in our forever home,
With still frames of our family together.

I know things have been tough,
But I know we're meant to be like your
Ticklish lips on my belly.

I promise we're meant to be,
And nobody can tell me differently.

You're the wolf and I'm the moon.
You're the sea and I'm the shore.
You're the glove and I'm the hand.
We fit together perfectly.

I'm sorry I'm so difficult to deal with,
I promise I'm not trying to be.

I can't lie, I haven't been okay,
And neither have you.

I can't explain all of these thoughts in
My head, but listen when I tell you this:

I'm not giving up, and I'll be darned if
This doesn't work out.

But I'm here to love you,
I'm here to breathe you in.

I'm here to be the reason you've
Been looking for, in order to stay
Alive in this cruel world.

Because God knows, you're the biggest
Reason I have.

You're the past, you're the present,
You're the future too.

You are the one I wrote about for years.
You are the one that always saved me in my
Nightmares.
You are the one that I wanted to hold me
As I'd cry myself to sleep once again.

I cannot thank you enough for all you've
Given up on so we can be together.
But please don't let that effort go to waste.

Because I won't stop loving you,
Even if you walk away.

Let Me Read You

I wanna know everything
About you.
Like how you're scared of dying,
But some days, it's all you want to do.
I want to know what it's like inside your mind
When the days are dragging on too long,
Or flying by in the blink of an eye.
I want to know what the butterflies in your
Tummy look like. How fast do they flutter
When you rest your head upon my chest
To listen to my heart beating?
I want to know what horrors you faced before
Meeting me, so I know what I'm trying to
Help heal.

I know there is yellow in your eyes,
Which you used to hate.
I know there are times
When the world is moving far too fast for you,
But other times, it couldn't spin quickly enough.
I know you hate when I nag about your driving.
I know that coffee and witnessing my eyes
Opening are your two favourite things
About morning.

I want to know what makes you find peace
Within yourself during stormy weather.
I want to know why you're so persistent on
The idea of loving me.
Did you manifest this, too?

Always Wait It Out

I plug in the fan and the extension cord,
Leave the phone charger on the bed
So the cats won't chew it.
I turn the night light on too so I feel safer,
And out of habit, I suppose.
I walk past my pills sitting freely on the dresser,
And slip into bed; not even glancing
At them.

You call on me, "Sweetie?"

I stir for a second. "Yea?" I call back.

"Can you come here?"

Instantly, I'm on my feet again and practically
Hopping/skipping my way over.

"He needs me," I think, "I'm needed."

Baby- our angel-haired, blue eyed, sweetie pie
Kitten,
Had sliced up your finger.
You're allergic to cats, so this is a problem.
You ask me to grab tape and bring it near.
Once you bandage it up,
You ask me to kiss it.
For a second, I think about how every
Kid I've ever worked with, has probably asked
Me to kiss a booboo better,
And then I thought about our future kids.
Ones that, if I actually go through with this,
Won't exist,
But if I don't do it,
They hopefully will exist.

I thought about how Evelyn's eyelashes are
Going to be just as long as daddy's, when
You closed your eyelids to kiss me.
I think about how Jace's smile will look just
Like mine, crooked and shy

I see them disappear before my eyes.
I see you finding another love.
I see me in the ground, dirt packed over
What's left of me.
What I mean by, what's left of me, is
My soul will have gone on to another
Realm, we'll call it.
Just a really deep delta wave, my love.
Pay no mind to the demons in your head.
The ones that are roaring louder now
That I'm not at your shoulder.
But please know, I love you...so much.

I see everything tonight. I see all of my
Mistakes and wrong doings.
I see how much I'm hurting.
Hurting like, I lay in an empty bathtub
Tonight and
Had a flashback while being in my
Safest space.
I couldn't breathe, I was literally erupting
And shaking like a volcano on boom-day,
And I couldn't get any words out.
I texted you, because apparently that's
The only thing I'm capable of doing when
Stoned and panicked.
Oh yea, sorry mum, I'm not sober.

You finally answer and I cry inside.
I say I'm sorry for bugging.
I see how out of shape I've gotten, sitting
Down in skin tight, high waisted hippie pants.
I feel how gross my teeth are from smoking
And skipping brushing them today.
I feel how broken I am inside.
I feel how guilty I am too.
Guilty for putting you through this;
The drama of it all.

For not being able to clean everything up
When you weren't home.
For napping instead with a guided meditation
Playing through the TV.
I hear you unlock the front door,
Am I dreaming?
No, I feel a kiss on my forehead. It's you.

I zone back in.
Baby is asleep at my hip.
I am alone otherwise.

All I have to say is I love you,
You're the love of my life, you are
Everything I ever, and continue to dream of,
You are the protector I always deserved,
You are the comedy show I longed to
Sit front row at,
You are the reason I stayed so long.
You are the reason I gave my all.
You are the reason I felt so alive.
Thank you, I love you,
I'm sorry.

"11:11," I say, "Make a wish."

"Oh God, if only I could think of one," you joke,
While reminiscing over your pain from the cat
Scratches. You say "oh hey, but at least we have
All day together tomorrow!"

I forgot our plans.

Our plans.

Maybe that's just enough reason to wait it
Out.

A Letter to the Reader,

I thank you. Thank you for spending your valuable time reading about silly ol' me. Please, I ask for you to close this book and close part of yourself too. However, I hope more than anything, that you reopen these pages, and tend to your open gashes, as well. This book was written to heal myself, and hopefully someone else too. I hope to help a struggling 16 year old, 35 year old, and everyone in between; for you reading this is helping me heal too. Thank you for allowing me to do so. Thank you for letting me follow and achieve my dreams. Simply, thank you.

For more content and future book releases, follow Charlie Iris on Facebook and @charlie.iris.poetry on Instagram.

A Letter to My Lover
Copyright © 2023 by Charlie Iris
Illustrations © Rebecca MacDonald and Evelyn Ferris
All rights reserved. Printed in Canada.
No part of this book may be used or reproduced in any manner whatsoever without written permission except in case of brief quotations within critical articles and reviews.

www.ingramcontent.com/pod-product-compliance
Lightning Source LLC
Chambersburg PA
CBHW072100110526
44590CB00018B/3259